PERFORMANCE
EDITIONS

CHOPIN
SELECTED PRELUDES
Lower Intermediate to Intermediate Level

Edited and Recorded by Brian Ganz

To access companion recorded performances online, visit:
www.halleonard.com/mylibrary

Enter Code
2334-7655-7455-7469

Also available:
Chopin: Preludes (complete)
Edited and Recorded by Brian Ganz
Schirmer Performance Editions
HL00296523

On the cover:
The Composer Chopin Playing in the Salon of Prince Radziville in Berlin in 1829 (detail)
by Henry Siemiradzki
(ca. 1887)

© The Bridgeman Art Library/Getty Images

ISBN 978-1-4234-5523-3

G. SCHIRMER, *Inc.*

DISTRIBUTED BY

HAL•LEONARD®
CORPORATION
7777 W. BLUEMOUND RD. P.O. BOX 13819 MILWAUKEE, WI 53213

www.musicsalesclassical.com
www.halleonard.com

CONTENTS

The price of this publication includes access to companion recorded performances online, for download or streaming, using the unique code found on the title page. Visit **www.halleonard.com/mylibrary** and enter the access code.

HISTORICAL NOTES

LUDWIG VAN BEETHOVEN (1770-1827)

Beethoven and the Bagatelle

The title "Bagatelle" on a piece of music was first used by François Couperin (1668–1733) for a work in his tenth *Ordre*, published in 1717. *The New Grove Dictionary of Music and Musicians* defines the term specifically as "a trifle, a short piece of music in light vein."[1] While many other works with the title "Bagatelle" were written and published in the 18th and 19th centuries, those of Ludwig van Beethoven are surely the best-known. In all, he wrote 24 bagatelles catalogued as Op. 33, 119, and 126, and four separate bagatelles without opus numbers (WoO).

These magnificent shorter works encapsulate, and in many ways, summarize the musical characteristics of one of the most influential composers in history. While the larger works (such as the symphonies and sonatas) appropriately command a great amount of attention and most thoroughly reflect his genius, it may actually be easier to get an overview of his style by studying smaller works, such as these. In short-form works we find numerous characteristics of Beethoven's writing, seen quickly and succinctly.

Before discussing the individual pieces, it is important to see where they fit into the composer's output, and thereby learn what style of his writing they reflect. Beethoven's compositional career is traditionally divided into three periods, marking his evolution as a composer. The idea of three compositional periods was first proposed by Johann Schlosser, in his biography of Beethoven, published only a few months after the composer's death.[2] While many would debate the specific dates of each period, it can be approximated that the first ends around 1802, the second concludes by 1812, and the final period encompasses works written from 1813 until his death in 1827.

The first period could be called Beethoven's most "Classical" period, the time in which his works are essentially in line with the Viennese style at the turn of the century. Comparisons to the music of Haydn and Mozart are not uncommon. In the second period, we find the more adventurous or heroic style emerging, as seen in the Third Symphony ("Eroica"), the Fifth Symphony, and piano sonatas such as the "Waldstein," Op. 53, and the "Appassionata," Op. 57. The works of this period are the first to uniquely distinguish Beethoven's music from the expected temperament of Classicism, and are full of experimentation in form, color, and thematic development. In the final period, Beethoven's work is often referred to as introspective, reflecting a greater emotional turmoil in his life, and his isolated internal world of deafness. The Ninth Symphony and the last five piano sonatas were written during this time, and display in so many ways his search for new means of expression. Some of the more striking traits are his use of fugue and instrumental recitative. Today, as we look back over the course of music history, these last two periods seem to display a general move toward the Romantic era, with its increased expansiveness, rubato and accelerando, the passionate and the macabre, the ferocious and the delicate, the new heights and depths of individual musical expression. To hear some of the differences in these periods, I recommend listening—at one sitting—to one work from each period. Below are two suggested lists, with the date of completion in parentheses:

Sonatas

First period: Op. 2, No.1 in F minor (1795)

Second period: Op. 53 in C major, "Waldstein" (1804)

Third period: Op. 110 in A-flat major (1822)

Symphonies

First period: No. 1 in C major, Op. 21 (1800)

Second period: No. 5 in C minor, Op. 67 (1808)

Third period: No. 9 in D minor, Op. 125 (1824)

The seven bagatelles of Opus 33 were written and first performed between 1801 and 1802, at the approximate conclusion of the first period. At this time, Beethoven's hearing had already caused him difficulty for as many three years. Yet the music of this set is, as a whole, very bright and happy. It encompasses a wide range of technical difficulties. Four of the Opus 33 bagatelles are included in this edition.

Opus 119 includes eleven bagatelles (eight of which appear in this edition), completed and first performed between 1820 and 1822, in the middle of the final period. In general, these have a wider variety of styles than the earlier set, and a range of moods, from melancholy (No. 1) to restless (No.10).

Also included in this edition are two other bagatelles, WoO 60, and the famous "Für Elise", WoO 59. WoO 60 was composed in 1818; the details of WoO 59 are in the following section on the individual works.

—*Matthew Edwards*

The editor wishes to dedicate this edition to Robert McDonald, teacher, mentor, friend.

PERFORMANCE NOTES

In my edition of introductory Beethoven piano works *(Beethoven: Selected Piano Works, Schirmer Performance Editions)*, the great majority of the pieces are compositionally simpler than most of the bagatelles in this collection. With this selection of bagatelles, the complexities increase in all areas: technically, musically, and harmonically. Many of these works were written as teaching pieces, particularly those from Op. 119. The increased lengths of the pieces allow Beethoven's style to be more present. In order to understand more fully the value of these works to the progressing student, let's examine the three areas stated above.

Technique

Some of the more obvious difficulties include large leaps, double thirds, tremolo/Alberti figures, occasional brief passages of octaves in one hand, chromatic passagework, and large, full chords. Pianists learning these pieces will find a supple wrist, relaxed muscles, and well-balanced weight (arm/hand/finger) to be critical tools in navigating these challenges. These are excellent works to accompany a growing technical regimen.

Musical Issues

With a wider variety of technical issues, the performer may find it increasingly difficult to remain focused on expression. The musical aims and issues must be of primary importance, and should guide the performer's technical choices, rather than the technique dictating the interpretation. This is one reason that I strongly advocate studying the score away from the piano. Preferably, this would be done before the work is ever actually practiced on the keyboard, either by hearing it in your head, or listening to a recording while studying. Score study allows you to focus first on the shape and expression of the music, without letting your fingers get in the way. Once the musical path has begun to formulate in the mind, the technique will adjust more easily in pursuit of it.

The simple fact that Beethoven's style evolved can cause interpretive difficulties. It is not especially difficult to hear the distinctions between the Classical and the Romantic eras, but much of Beethoven's music falls squarely "in between" these, and will contain musical characteristics of both. As a simple example, the earlier works may be better played with a strict tempo, aligning with the Classical style; the later, more Romantic works will have room for more rubato, and/or greater freedom of tempo. It is important, therefore, to consider the date of composition as a musical plan is developed for these works.

Harmony

Tonal theory shows us that there are certain progressions of chords that are the most expected, or "natural." For example, the progression ii-V-I is one of the most common cadences in Western music; we expect the I chord to follow the ii and V. But if the final chord is vi, rather than I, then we have but one example of what I refer to as a "harmonic surprise." That specific progression, often called a "Deceptive Cadence," ends unexpectedly. All music contains surprises; Beethoven's middle and late period contain some particularly interesting ones. Many can be found in this selection of bagatelles. Be aware of where these exist in a work, and make a musical plan that displays the moment appropriately. Be careful not to over-emphasize, or the subtle surprise may turn into a sudden shock!

Notes on Performance Practice

Two issues must be discussed here, one concerning the piano of Beethoven's day, and the other, the execution of trills. The damper pedal is of particular concern, because the markings by Classical composers can occasionally seem impractical today. Beethoven made many pedal markings in his music, and used the damper pedal considerably in performance. According to Czerny, he used it "far more than is indicated in his works;" in one performance of the Piano Concerto in C minor, "he held the pedal through the *entire slow movement.*"[3] One must remember, however, that in the early 1800s the piano was strung with much thinner wire which did not vibrate for long.[4] Keep this in mind when interpreting Beethoven's pedal markings, particularly those held over several measures and/or harmonic changes. There are times when it is appropriate to insert additional pedal changes. Other options could include flutter pedal, half-pedal or even three-quarter pedal, which may help achieve the kind of sound actually intended. The *Bagatelle*, Op. 33, No. 7 is an example of the pedaling issue.

The most common question concerning trills is whether to begin on the given note, or on the note above. On the one hand, C.P.E. Bach (1714–1788) indicates that the trill should begin above, and indeed this was the common practice through the middle of the 18th century. By 1828, however, the pianist and composer Johann Nepomuk Hummel (1778–1837), in his book on piano playing, states clearly that the trill should begin on the main note.[5] It would seem that by the early 19th century the issue was in a variable state, with the common practice "transitioning" from beginning the trill above the note to on the note. Considering that these bagatelles were written between 1801 and 1822, we cannot be dogmatic about the beginning pitch of the trills. Either approach could be defended, but my preference in Op. 33, with their earlier date and tendency toward Classicism, is to begin the trills from the note above. In the later Op. 119 one would be more likely to begin trills on the principal note. Even with these suggestions, choices should be made for each individual work, rather than for the entire group.

Other Editorial Thoughts

The majority of the dynamic markings in this book are Beethoven's; added markings are in brackets. Op. 119 is particularly empty of original markings, but considering the pedagogic nature of this edition, a few have been suggested where appropriate. As carefully as he examined his scores before publication, we must assume that Beethoven intended the interpretation of this set to be more in the hands of the performer.

In general, I have attempted to suggest fingerings with the intermediate student in mind. Some fingerings are purely functional, to aid learning; some are specified for the sake of the musical line. When dealing with wider double notes and octaves, it is difficult to choose a fingering that works for everyone. In these cases, I have tried to find a middle ground, although sometimes to the detriment of the phrasing. As with any fingerings, they are suggestions only, to be tried first, and kept only if they allow success.

While many of Beethoven's sonatas lie well beyond the difficulties encountered in these bagatelles, I have drawn parallels where possible. It is important to see these works in relation to the larger output of Beethoven, and to see the similarities that exist. Additionally, in my experience, this type of comparison has often helped to pique a student's interest in a wider range of repertoire.

I hope that you find these comments and the recording helpful in the process of learning these wonderful works. The performances are born out my own study, experience, and teaching, but they are also the result of a particular spontaneous moment in time. It is that spontaneity of sudden inspiration, combined with careful planning and practice, that makes each musical performance unique and different. Use the recordings as perhaps a provocative guide to these works, but not as the definitive edition, as is no one recording.

The Individual Works

Bagatelle in A Minor, WoO 59, "Für Elise"

This timeless work, known around the world to piano students of every age, was not published until 1867, a full 40 years after Beethoven's death. The history of its composition is a bit unclear. It was written between 1808 and 1810; support for the latter date is drawn from the work's likely connection to Therese Malfatti, whose father was Beethoven's physician. Beethoven courted Therese, despite her apparent indifference towards him, and her parents clear opposition to the relationship.[6] In 1810, the relationship ended with a rejected marriage proposal. It is thought, however, that Beethoven wrote this work for a family gathering at the Malfatti home, and intended to give it to her as part of the marriage proposal. Originally titled "Für Therese," it is supposed to have been found in her home in a box of music after her death in 1851. Published much later by Ludwig Nohl, the inscription was misread—an understandable problem, considering Beethoven's notoriously difficult penmanship—and was published under its current well-known title.

Knowing this background information helps us to see a bit more depth in the work, as we consider the possibility that Beethoven was aware the relationship was not going to end in marriage, as he had hoped. The opening should be thoughtful and possibly melancholy, with a graceful accompaniment in the left hand. The two-note figure of E and D-sharp, such an important element of this opening melody, has the sound of uncertainty to it; particularly in the transition back to the melody in mm. 14-15. Perhaps the second section is a reminder of happier times, with its brighter melody and dance-like accompaniment. In mm. 32-36, take care not to let the right hand become too "violent", but work for a gentle sound by keeping the fingers relaxed, particularly the fifth finger in measure 32. The third section, beginning in measure 61, reflects the stress and tension of his emotional struggle at the time. The repeated 16ths of the left hand should never be static dynamically, but should follow the musical leading of the right hand melody. Take particular care on this point when there are two notes in the accompaniment, as in mm. 66-68. Measure 73 contains the best musical surprise in the work, as the tonal center suddenly rises from a minor to B-flat major—either a slight accent or *rallentando* will draw our attention to this. In measure 79, avoid any accent on the first note of the triplets. Move the hand swiftly and freely to each new position, without a "crash-landing" when the thumb crosses under. The final statement of the main theme almost fades into the distance; be careful not to make the ending too dramatic or too loud.

Bagatelle in B-flat Major, WoO 60

This is a very playful work, with frequent shifts of mood or character. Keeping the 16th notes short will give it energy, and will enhance the contrast with the more *legato* writing, particularly in mm. 14-25. In measure 18, although the two notes are divided between the hands, they should sound as if they are one voice, answered by the "real" right hand voice in the next measure.

Bagatelle in B-flat Major, WoO 60: mm. 18-20

Also, be as exact as possible with all of the rests, whether they are quarters, as in mm. 8-9, or 16ths as in measure 27 and others. The F in the left hand at measure two seems a bit out of place harmonically, but the slightest bit of emphasis on the F in measure one and measure two will help clarify his intended chord. Other harmonic surprises exist in this work, in particular, measures 20 and 21. A slight *rallentando* going into measure 21 will help ease the "shock" of the key change, allowing the E-double flat to "become" the D-natural in our ears. The frequent key changes are reminiscent of the first movement of the *Sonata in E Minor*, Op. 90, which establishes or implies seven tonal centers in the first 45 measures.

Bagatelle in C Major, Op. 33, No. 2

This work is most nearly a rondo, as it follows the scheme of ABACA. The section in minor at measure 17 is the B section, and the trio at measure 49 is the C. The purity of the form becomes a bit muddled, however, when he begins a variation of A at measure 95, and follows that with a coda (measure 111) to close the work. The opening A theme is bright and cheerful, with a good harmonic surprise in mm. 5-7. We might have expected him to close this eight-bar phrase on a C major chord—the tonic—but by avoiding that, Beethoven is forcing us to think of the longer line. We must consider all 16 measures to be one long pursuit of that elusive tonic cadence, which finally appears at the end. Be careful not to accent the first note of the motive in measure 1 and elsewhere; Beethoven is quite specific as to the dynamics here.

The warm *legato* of the B section provides a good contrast to the staccato in the A section. If possible, play the octaves with the suggested fingering. The left hand should generate a subtle energy, never overpowering the melody. The C section presents the greatest technical difficulty of the work, in the form of double-thirds passagework. A fingering here has been suggested, but as is always the case with fingerings, one should be chosen that best fits the unique traits and skills of each pianist. Above all, the goal for these two passages of thirds is a smooth and even sound, without noticeable accent or dotted rhythm. This section sounds much fuller than the A section, utilizing the lower register a great deal more, and a generally wide distance between the hands. Be sure to draw the listener's attention to the voice that contains the melodic material, as it switches from hand to hand. The best example of this is in mm. 61-70. The variation and coda increase the rhythmic energy of the original idea.

In measure 131 he tests our sense of meter, as the 3/4 nearly gives way to 2/4. One should be careful not to attempt to "clarify" the 3/4 by emphasizing beat one of each measure. The trio section of the *Sonata in E-flat Major, Op. 31, No. 3*, contains a similar section of 3/4 meter, and yet the chords sound briefly as if they are in 2/4.

Sonata in E-flat Major, Op. 31, No. 3:
third movement, mm. 24-31

Bagatelle in A Major, Op. 33, No. 4

An excellent study in polyphony and careful voicing, this lovely work has perhaps more musical difficulties than technical ones. There are no fewer than three lines that seek our attention in the opening measures; how much emphasis each one gets provides numerous interpretive possibilities. Changing the emphasis slightly can add contrast to the repeated sections. The middle voice of the right hand seems initially the more melodic voice; the upper voice appears more decorative, being rather "bell-like" on the E before it rises stepwise to the A in measure 2. Always keep in mind the third line, in the left hand, which provides some beautiful harmonic counterpoint, particularly beginning at measure 9. The trill in measure 2 could be executed with the third and fourth fingers, so that the thumb can hold the quarter-note B, and thereby resolve more smoothly to the following A. Using the second and third fingers could make the trill easier, but may require the thumb to let go of the B quite early, thereby breaking the melodic connection. If your hands are large enough, the B could be held by the left hand, so the right hand can focus exclusively on the trill.

Bagatelle in A Major, Op. 33, No. 4: m. 2

In the B section, which begins at measure 16, the left hand melody must be as *legato* as possible, while the right provides a gentle accompaniment. In mm. 24-26, since the left hand is not changing pitch, give a slight emphasis to the right hand notes that do change, the C, B, A, and G-sharp. In the variation of A that begins at measure 38, relax the hand for the trill, so as not to overemphasize it. A little bit of pedal may help these trills, but not so much that it blurs the right hand 16ths.

Bagatelle in D Major, Op. 33, No. 6

Both phrases of the opening period are nearly identical (mm. 1-8), distinguished only by a change of register, and a single note change in the approach to the cadence. These eight bars should not sound static, however, as the forward motion of the first phrase is provided by the right hand 16th notes at the first cadence point. The final phrase sounds conclusive simply by settling on the quarter. This small difference is critical in the shaping of the larger eight-bar period, so that it indeed sounds like a single long melodic breath, rather than two repeated phrases.

The trills in this work should most likely begin on the upper note, and consist of a total of four 32nd notes. This will help keep the following 16th notes distinct from the trill itself. See the "Notes on Performance Practice" for further information on trills in Beethoven's time.

The middle section, beginning at measure 21, contains a brief but exciting section of modulation to F-sharp minor. Beethoven takes the first five notes of the opening melody, and uses that motive to lead us away from D major. Each re-statement of the motive—sounding like a series of questions—rises dynamically, until arriving at the key of F-sharp minor in measure 28.

In measure 38, the low 16th note A in the right hand may prove to be quite a challenge. A possible solution, rather than spending an inordinate amount of time working on this, would be to take that A with the left hand, and let the right hand resume the line on the following B.

Bagatelle in D Major, Op. 33, No. 6: m. 38

In this case, care must be taken not to accent the A, but practice to make the line sound uniform, as if it were only one hand.

The variations in the return of A are a good exercise in lyrical chromatic playing, most of the alterations being neighbor notes added to the original melody. The fingerings suggested may require some practice, but should be helpful in managing the *legato* of the line.

Bagatelle in A-flat Major, Op. 33, No. 7

A high-spirited work full of suspense and energy, this bagatelle is reminiscent of the famous "Waldstein" sonata, Op. 53. Perhaps it would be more accurate to say that this piece anticipates the sonata, as it was completed in 1802, two years prior to the larger work. The first similarities are right at the beginning, where the quarters of the bagatelle establish a quick and persistent rhythmic bass line. The sonata's opening eighth notes have a similar relentless sound.

Sonata in C Major, Op. 53: first movement, mm. 1-3

Bagatelle in A-flat Major, Op. 33, No. 7: mm. 1-5

In measure 45 of the bagatelle, the added eighth notes are comparable to the 16ths in the right hand of the sonata. An additional similarity occurs between mm. 21-37 of the bagatelle, and the main theme of the third movement of the "Waldstein." When played according to his pedaling and dynamics, the sonata passage sounds somewhat ethereal, as the two harmonies gently mingle with each other.

Sonata in C Major, Op. 53: third movement, mm. 1-4

Bagatelle in A-flat Major, Op. 33, No. 7: mm. 21-28

This sound can be achieved by using half-pedal or three-quarter pedal, where the dampers only partially dampen the strings. The low A-flat keeps the passage grounded in the tonic key, just as the low C does in the sonata.

At the *Presto* marking, this work is one of the more difficult in this collection. To begin, the wrist must remain supple and relaxed throughout in order to play the quarters. One suggestion is to play each measure with a "down-up-up" motion in the hand to keep tension at a minimum, yet without accenting beat one. In particular, keep a relaxed left hand for the tremolos in measures 101 and 121. Metronome practice is critical for this piece, and you should play it no faster than you can successfully navigate the left hand of mm. 145-150.

One of the major difficulties in this work is avoiding unnecessary accents that result when a quick change of register is required. For example, in measure 48, the right hand has a good distance to travel, and must also switch quickly from accompaniment to melody. It is most important that the final beat is not accented, by "crash-landing" on the treble A-flat. Think of it as if you are moving your hand as fast as possible to a position just above the note, rather than actually on it; once you are there, the finger simply drops into the note. In that way, the momentum is stopped prior to playing the note, rather than by the note itself.

Bagatelle in G Minor, Op. 119, No. 1

This work is comprised of two equally lovely melodies (at measure 1 and measure 17), with appropriate contrasts of key center and articulation. Too much emphasis on the staccatos in the opening melody will break the phrase into segmented motives. Rather, keep them gentle, almost cautious, focusing always on the melody that exists over the staccato articulation. For the middle section, he chooses E-flat major instead of the relative major, B-flat, and presents us with the lyrical second theme. While effort should clearly be made to keep the melody prominent, also watch the movements of the inner voices as well, particularly when they move by half or whole steps, as in mm. 21-22. A little attention to these will keep the accompaniment from sounding like a plain set of chords under a pretty melody.

I have marked the phrasing in mm. 52-64 so as to reflect the feeling of 2/4 within the triple meter. Do not accent the first note of each phrase, as the writing itself makes the "meter change" clear. Also, in mm. 58-63, the emphasis should initially be on the left hand, become more equal between the hands in mm. 60-62, and shift entirely to the right hand in mm. 62-64.

Bagatelle in D Major, Op. 119, No. 3

This work could nearly be titled "Scherzo," as it certainly seems like Beethoven is joking with us at both the beginning and the ending of this work. In particular, the right hand should almost literally "toss" the opening motive out to the audience, in both gesture and sound. Be careful of Beethoven's pedal marking here, similar to the one discussed in the *Bagatelle*, Op. 33, No. 7. In this case, perhaps a half-pedal would work best, to keep it from sounding too muddy. The middle section is an excellent study for both tremolo and Alberti bass. While there is the real potential for this to sound much more serious than the opening, there is room for it to be light-hearted—even slightly sarcastic—and always full of bright energy. Don't over-emphasize the large chords, or they may sound harsh. In measure 54, be sure to give the two eighth rests their exact value, so that the final figure is even more surprising—the last laugh in this humorous work.

Bagatelle in A Major, Op. 119, No. 4

With its detailed melodic accompaniment in the left hand and delicate inner voices, the performer must take care to shape all three lines in this bagatelle, shifting the focus from one to another as the opening phrases repeat.

The *Andante cantabile* tempo Beethoven assigns to this piece aptly describes the exquisitely lyrical nature of this beautiful solo, and the 16th notes in the B section emphasize the need for a slower tempo throughout. They should be played at an unhurried pace so that they contribute to the reflective mood of the work. Observe the two-note slurs precisely, but without a sharp, *staccato* release of the second note, so that each passage still sounds nearly *legato*.

Bagatelle in C Minor, Op. 119, No. 5

Dense chords and sharp rhythms give this bagatelle a bold, almost militaristic sound—appropriate for the "Risoluto" marking. The grace notes will add to that character best if they are played quite closely to the following notes, regardless of the tempo chosen. Keep in mind that a 6/8 meter should feel like a 2/4, with the first beat having the primary accent, and the fourth beat having a secondary accent. If all six beats are of equal strength, it will sound too heavy and thick. Because of the forceful nature of the left hand, it may be best to practice the right hand alone first, so that the phrasing can be better understood. After that, add the left hand, and let it be guided dynamically by the line of the right.

Be careful not to let the right hand unnecessarily accent notes when the line suddenly changes register, as in mm. 8-9 and similar passages. Keep measure 16 and following very strict, although a slight pause between the last two notes could give better finality to the work.

Bagatelle in C Major, Op. 119, No. 8

Another excellent polyphonic study, the performer must attempt to keep all four lines in mind. Similar polyphonic difficulties can be seen in Rondo movement of the *Sonata in G Major*, Op. 31, No. 1. The fingerings provided in the score may be tricky, and include finger exchanges, and unusual crossings. In spite of the difficulty, however, the given fingering should help you to hold all notes for their full indicated value, and to maintain the continuity of the lines. The pedal may at times help, but be careful that it doesn't make the lines muddy and unclear. The melody is of primary importance, but observe the chromatic and diatonic stepwise movement in the lower voices. A good suggestion for understanding these multiple lines would be to play through each one individually several times from beginning to end. After that, use both hands to play the two lines of the right hand, then the two lines of the left, observing and listening to the way they interact together. Once all parts are played together after this preparation, the lines will be much better understood. You may yet find a place or two where a certain note might be better played by the opposite hand indicated. An example is measure 8, on the final beat. It may be easier to play the left hand D with the right hand, and the right hand B with the left.

Bagatelle in C Major, Op. 119, No. 8: m. 8

Such note exchanges may not be exactly what Beethoven wrote, but is the better choice if it makes the passage more musical.

Bagatelle in A Minor, Op. 119, No. 9

This brief, graceful waltz presents many challenges for the intermediate performer. In the fingerings, you will see that the right-hand eighth note E in measure 1 is assigned to finger 2, but the thumb is also given in parenthesis as an alternate fingering.

Bagatelle in A Minor, Op. 119, No. 9: mm. 1-2, r.h.

Those with smaller hands should clearly choose the thumb, and possibly even use it again for the second eighth note in measure 2. But when the second finger plays this note, it becomes readily apparent that the entire arpeggiated figure consists of two four-note chords in succession: a first-inversion A minor chord, followed by a root-position A minor chord.

Bagatelle in A Minor, Op. 119, No. 9: mm. 1-2, r.h.

Therefore, using the second finger in measure 1 allows the performer to make only one position change for the figure—not counting the final E and C—as opposed to three position changes when the thumb is used in measure 1. Both fingerings work, and the performer should choose the one that elicits the most graceful sound. The bass-note downbeats throughout should be supportive, but never heavy.

Bagatelle in A Major, Op. 119, No. 10

Of all the *Bagatelles,* this one most definitely fulfills its designation as a "trifle," although not at all in a negative sense. Barely begun before it ends abruptly, Beethoven gives us a tidy and compact repeated period with a coda in a mere 13 measures of music. Its brief life is spirited and energetic. It may be better thought of as a 4/4 meter, so as to keep the phrases from becoming too segmented. In that way, beat "one" falls at the beginning of the odd-numbered measures.

You may find the syncopation of the left hand to be difficult, particularly at higher speeds. Keep the right hand prominent in your own ears to keep from getting "off-balance" rhythmically. Careful practice with the metronome will also help.

Bagatelle in B-flat Major, Op. 119, No. 11

This stately and lyrical bagatelle is an appropriate conclusion to Opus 119. The lower part in the right hand provides a very subtle counterpoint to the melody, particularly in mm. 15-18. In mm. 11-18, care should be taken to observe the left hand rests as much as possible, so as to allow the most contrast between the hands. The melody and its accompaniment bear a certain resemblance to first statement of the theme in the *Andante* movement of the *Sonata in E Major,* Op. 109.

Sonata in E Major, Op. 109: third movement, mm. 1-4

—*Matthew Edwards*

Notes

1. Brown, Maurice J.E.: "Bagatelle", Grove Music Online (Accessed 6/1/07), <http://www.grovemusic.com.ezproxy.aacc.edu>

2. Kerman, Joseph and Alan Tyson, et. al: "Beethoven, Ludwig van; The 'three periods'", Grove Music Online (Accessed 6/10/07), <http://www.grovemusic.com.ezproxy.aacc.edu>

3. Schoenberg, Harold: *The Great Pianists.* New York: Simon & Schuster, Inc., 1987.

4. In fact, pianos built before 1825 had wooden frames, which were not capable of handling the tension of today's thicker strings. The thicker the string, the longer the resonance. A simple illustration of this on a modern piano is the rapid decay of the sound when a very high note is struck, versus the lengthy decay of a bass note.

5. Brown, Clive: "Ornaments: Trills, turns and related ornaments." Grove Music Online (Accessed 6/24/07) <http://www.grovemusic.com.ezproxy.aacc.edu>

6. Solomon, Maynard. *Beethoven,* 2nd ed. New York: Schirmer Trade Books, 2001.

Bagatelle in A Minor
"Für Elise"

Ludwig van Beethoven
WoO 59

Poco moto

*Traditionally played as D; E in the autograph and first edition.

*See footnote on p. 12.

*See footnote on p. 12.
**Some editions have:

*See footnote on p. 12.

**Alternately:

Bagatelle in B-flat Major

Ludwig van Beethoven
WoO 60

Bagatelle in C Major

Ludwig van Beethoven
Op. 33, No. 2

Scherzo allegro

Bagatelle in A Major

Ludwig van Beethoven
Op. 33, No. 4

Bagatelle in D Major

Ludwig van Beethoven
Op. 33, No. 6

Allegretto quasi Andante*
Con una certa espressione parlante

*"*quasi Andante*" in the original edition only; missing in the autograph.

*See note on page 8 for an alternate fingering for this passage.

Bagatelle in A-flat Major

Ludwig van Beethoven
Op. 33, No. 7

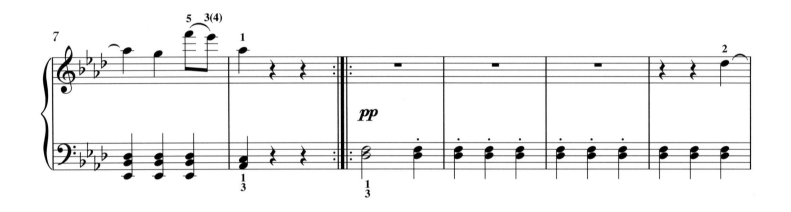

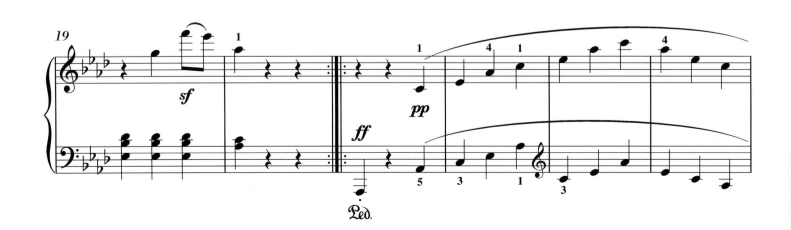

Bagatelle in G Minor

Ludwig van Beethoven
Op. 119, No. 1

Allegretto

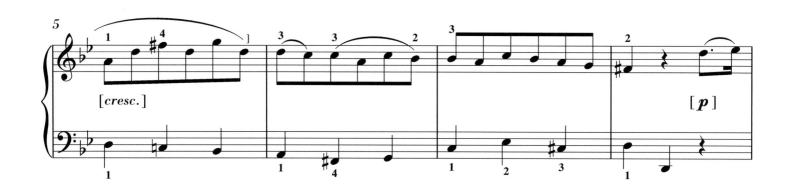

Bagatelle in D Major

Ludwig van Beethoven
Op. 119, No. 3

à l'Allemande

**Da capo sin' al segno 𝄋
ed allora la Coda**

Coda

Bagatelle in A Major

Ludwig van Beethoven
Op. 119, No. 4

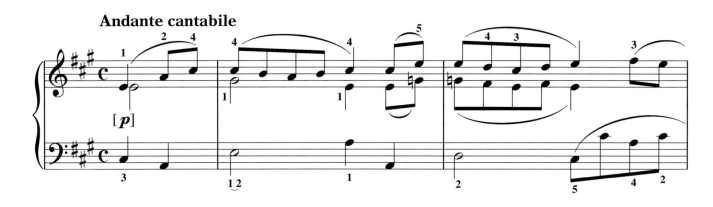

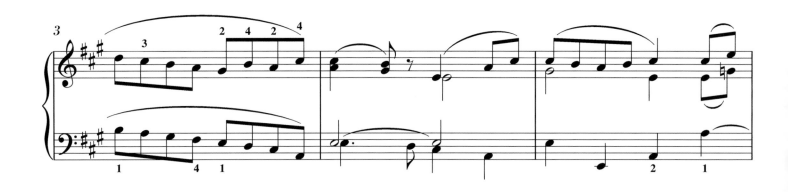

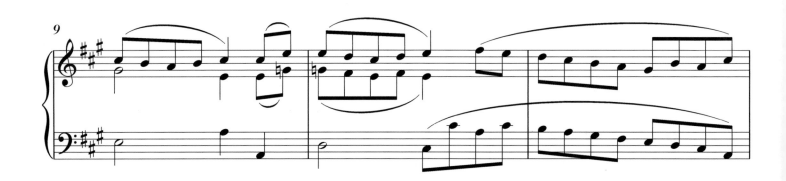

Bagatelle in C Minor

Ludwig van Beethoven
Op. 119, No. 5

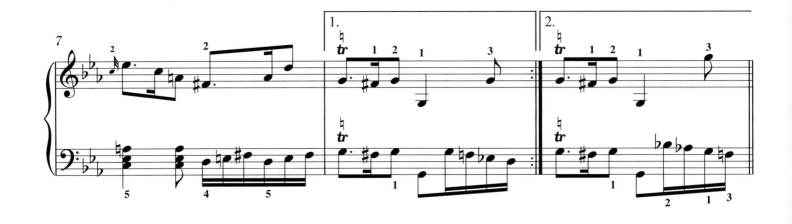

Bagatelle in C Major

Ludwig van Beethoven
Op. 119, No. 8

Moderato cantabile

* The two bass quarter-notes *d* and *d♯* according to the
first editions; the autograph has a half note *d*.

Bagatelle in A Minor

Ludwig van Beethoven
Op. 119, No. 9

Vivace moderato

Bagatelle in A Major

Ludwig van Beethoven
Op. 119, No. 10

Allegramente

Bagatelle in B-flat Major

Ludwig van Beethoven
Op. 119, No. 11

Andante, ma non troppo

* **C** according to first editions; autograph: ¢

ABOUT THE EDITOR

BRIAN GANZ

Brian Ganz is widely regarded as one of the leading pianists of his generation. After he performed the Preludes in an all-Chopin recital in Washington D.C., the Washington Post declared, "One comes away from a recital by pianist Brian Ganz not only exhilarated by the power of the performance but also moved by his search for artistic truth."

Mr. Ganz was winner of one of two First Grand Prizes awarded in the 1989 Marguerite Long-Jacques Thibaud International Piano Competition in Paris. That same year, he won a Beethoven Fellowship awarded by the American Pianists Association, and in 1991 he was a silver medalist with third prize in the Queen Elisabeth of Belgium International Piano Competition. After his performance in the finals of the Brussels competition, the critic for La Libre Belgique wrote, "We don't have the words to speak of this fabulous musician who lives music with a generous urgency and brings his public into a state of intense joy."

He has appeared as soloist with such orchestras as the St. Louis Symphony, the St. Petersburg (Russia) Philharmonic, the City of London Sinfonia, L'Orchestre Lamoureux, and L'Orchestre Philharmonique de Monte Carlo, and has performed under the baton of such conductors as Leonard Slatkin, Mstislav Rostropovich, and Pinchas Zukerman. He made his recording debut in 1992 for the Gailly label in Belgium, and his recordings of Chopin and Dutilleux have been released on the Accord label in Paris. In 2001, he began a project with Maestoso Records in which he will record the complete works of Chopin.

Mr. Ganz is a graduate of the Peabody Conservatory of Music, where he studied with Leon Fleisher. Earlier teachers include Ylda Novik and the late Claire Deene. Gifted as a teacher himself, Mr. Ganz is Artist-in-Residence at St. Mary's College of Maryland, where he has been a member of the piano faculty since 1986. In 2000, he joined the piano faculty of the Peabody Conservatory.